TENDING GRIEF

A Guide for Your Journey

Jack Wiens

Copyright © 2016 Jack Wiens
Ashland, Oregon
ISBN-13: 978-1533240941

Book design and computer production by
Patty Arnold, *Menagerie Design & Publishing*

Contents

Foreword	4–5
Introduction	6
Defining Grief and What to Expect	9
What About Those Stages?	17
Faith and Grief	20
Sudden Loss	21
Anticipated Loss	22
Conscious Grieving	23
Finding Support	24
A Parent's Grief	25
Helping Ourselves on the Journey of Grief	26
1. Honor Your Feelings	27
2. Make a Time and Place	27
3. Triggers	28
4. Expressing Feelings	29
5. Comforting Yourself	30
6. Asking for What You Need	30
7. Anger	32
8. Regrets and Shoulds	33
9. Give Yourself a Break	34
10. Commemorate Your Loss	35
11. Invite Peace In	36
Deciding If You Need Professional Help	38
About Medication	40
Abuse and Unfinished Business	41–42
Forgiveness	43
Suicide and Violent Death	44
Happier Feelings	46
Grieving Fully	46
The Ultimate Questions	47
Do's and Don'ts for helping someone who is grieving	48
Signs that someone might need more help than you can provide	49
A Quick Guide to Grief Tending	50
About the Author/Illustrator	51

Foreword

Dear Sweet Sister, dear Beloved Brother, dear unknown, but not unloved, Companion on this Human Journey...

Every part of my being opens to you now if you have found your way to this book during a time of desolation and mourning—or in a moment when you are watching someone else, someone for whom you would give your life, being ravaged by the raw, scorching experience of deep and unremitting grief.

No one has to tell you that there is nothing in the human encounter more rending of the heart, traumatizing to the mind, or producing of desperate questioning and searching of the soul, than the merciless bereavement that can follow overwhelming, crushing loss. And when what has been lost cannot in any way be replaced, ever, or even hope to be duplicated, even in modified form, the level of devastation can seem impossible to overcome.

Yet the blessed balm of healing is available to us still, and the life and work of Jack Wiens, and others like him throughout the world who have dedicated their lives to offering caring and compassion when comfort seems so elusive, is proof of it.

Here, in *Tending Our Grief*, is more than just commiseration, more than consolation and condolence, but practical and immediately applicable answers to the aching question, "How can the pain of this Finality finally end?"

It was Dr. Elisabeth Kübler-Ross, for whom I worked as a member of her personal staff, who taught me that grief is a natural emotion and a blessing; the part of us that allows us to not only feel, but to express (that is, to press out, to extract, thus to release) indescribable and debilitating sadness. But one may need help along the way. One may need tools, methods, and guidance in how to use them. For the movement through and beyond grief is not necessarily automatic, and grief that is not expressed, not pushed out or released, can turn into chronic depression, a very unnatural emotion.

I can tell you today that not since my work with Elisabeth have I seen such gently healing, insightfully hopeful, and profoundly helpful suggestions for dealing with loss than are found in Tending Our Grief. Thank you, Jack Wiens, for the remarkable, sensitive, and wonderfully constructive guidance you have offered in this writing.

And to anyone grieving today, know you have been led to the right place as you hold this book. It is not by happenstance or coincidence that you should find yourself here. I believe you have been placed here in answer to your inner call for help. Know, now, that your call has been heard.

~ Neale Donald Walsch
author of *Conversations with God*
and *Home with God in a Life That Never Ends*

Introduction

This book springs from my own experience of grief. I've counseled many grieving people...and

I am grieving. After forty-two years of marriage, my wife and I divorced. This loss has been the most painful and disorienting one of my life. Even after a few years now, I still grieve. My life has gone on. Good things have happened. I have been happy, even while being sad. I am learning that life is complex and we always have cause for tears, laughter, sadness, joy and gratitude. This is the lesson grief has slowly been teaching me.

Our culture doesn't really do grief well. In fact, we don't really deal with death very directly. We don't like to say someone died. We say they passed away or left us. Our portrayals of grief in the movies and media are rare and usually not too helpful. The impression given is that grief is a much shorter process than it actually is. Funerals, our main ritual for grieving, are usually quite orderly,

somber and subdued affairs, suggesting, unfortunately, that this is how to grieve. Grief can take a long time, slowly seeping into our consciousness, or can hit us like a tsunami. For some, grief can be a calm, sad-but-sweet experience of letting go. For most, however, it is a rougher ride, a journey through uncharted, unpredictable waters. One thing is certain: sooner or later, no matter what our age, gender, race, religion, or status, we all will experience loss.

This little book is offered as a guide through this emotional maze, not because you need to be "cured" of grief, but rather encouraged to fully enter into it as a normal, natural response to losing someone or something you love. It is about my own experience and that of many others. I think it will be about yours, too. My hope is you will find some helpful nuggets of truth, inspiration, comfort and even a chuckle along the way. We are in this together. You are not alone. You can grieve... and grieve well. — Jack Wiens, M.A.

Grief
is a normal,
natural response to loss.

It involves our whole being, our emotions, mind, body and spirit. It changes us in unpredictable ways and can take years to work through.

If your loved one has died, the depth of grief is directly related to the depth of love. If the loss you have experienced is a divorce, it can feel very much like a death. Or you might be dealing with the loss of a job, moving from home, a change in health, aging, the death of a pet, friends leaving. You might be grieving about our global losses or ungrieved losses from your past or your ancestors.

Most of us are not at all prepared for the grief experience. It is unlike anything we have known.

Initial grief can feel like numbness, like your mind and emotions have disengaged. This is a temporary condition that is built-in protection we humans have. It allows us to slowly ease into this unwanted reality. It is especially common when the loss is sudden and unexpected.

Our mind is being pushed to accept a painful reality it does not want to accept...

Sometimes the shock and numbness turns into denial...

A person might stay in denial a very long time until they have developed enough support and coping skills to allow them to deal directly with their grief. But over time, the grief that is bottled-up inside and held in the body can take a toll on physical and emotional health. The denied grief might finally be experienced even years later when a new loss is encountered. This compounded grief can be intense.

> *Not all grief starts with numbness or denial. Sometimes it begins with a confusing flood of emotions.*

This is a very common feeling when people are grieving. You are NOT going crazy. You are GRIEVING.

This too is a common fear. The feelings are so intense that it feels like a dam is about to break and you will be swept away in a flood of unending tears. But you won't. You will be able to stop. You can take care of yourself through this grief. You can do it consciously and you can love yourself as you make this journey...AND you don't have to make it alone.

What you can expect is the
UNEXPECTED!

Grief tends to come in unpredictable

waves of emotion that can be extremely disorienting.

Just when you think you are done
with those waves...

You might ride an emotional rollercoaster...
that can feel out of control and be very confusing.

Elisabeth Kübler-Ross, in her pioneering work, identified five stages dying people go through: denial, anger, bargaining, depression and acceptance. It is true the same stages might be experienced by those who grieve, however, it's not really helpful to set up an expectation that grief will follow any predictable order. Within one day you might experience all the stages in any order.

So when the waves of emotion hit or you experience big drops or twists of the "Amazing Grief Coaster" just know this is normal for the grief journey. Lovingly allow yourself to feel what you feel. Name the feelings. Speak them. Write them. Sit with them until you're ready to move on. These, too, will pass.

For awhile it might be difficult to relate to the world around you. You might feel detached or alienated from it

When hurting so badly because of your loss, the world feels so different. It seems impossible, even rude, that "normal" life just goes on around you as if nothing has happened! We imagine that our suffering is obvious to everyone, but it is not. Conditioning about being strong and in control may enable you to cover your pain very well, leading others to think that you are just fine. It's really okay to tell people what you are feeling. It is okay to cry. If the tears start to flow in the bank or grocery store, so what? If you feel the need to explain, simply say, "I'm grieving." You have a right to feel and to let it show.

Grief is an expression of Love.
    If you love deeply, you grieve deeply.

FAITH AND GRIEF

If a loved one died and you are a person of faith, you might question how your beliefs are being reflected in your grieving. Some well-meaning believers might say something like, "you should rejoice knowing your loved one is in a better place." Or you might be telling yourself you should be joyful instead of sad. You might have a strong belief that your loved one is safe with God in a beautiful heaven. You might believe with certainty that you will see them again someday. While this is a comfort, you may still be sad they are not with you now. You simply may miss their physical presence, which is a normal human response, not a lack of faith. Even Jesus wept when he heard of the death of his friend Lazarus. Our response to loss can be both a strong affirmation of faith and a full expression of grief with all its emotions. It might be helpful to talk with one of your faith's leaders about this issue.

If your loss is a sudden one, you might experience your grief differently than if the loss is gradual, as in a long terminal illness.

SUDDEN LOSS
might feel like a punch in the gut!

It will take time to get through the initial shock and confusion. Gradually, as the reality of your loss sinks in, you will likely experience all the feelings that come with grief.

ANTICIPATED LOSS

If a loved one is diagnosed with a terminal illness and is ill for an extended time, your grief will likely begin before your loved one actually dies. Your mind and heart gradually begin to accept the reality and prepare for letting go. When you care for someone and they are suffering, it is understandable to want the suffering to be over. A long-term illness can drain the emotional and physical resources of everyone who cares. You begin to grieve the loss of the person they once were. When death comes it can bring a confusing mix of feelings.

I feel GUILTY about feeling relieved.

The relief you feel is not about losing your loved one. It is about their suffering being over. Just acknowledge the guilt and let it go.

CONSCIOUS GRIEVING

When we consciously tend to our own grief we might find this opens us up to unexpressed grief we have been carrying for many years. Grief about losses in our past that could include things we needed but never got, traumas we experienced and so on.

We might even get in touch with grief we have carried from our ancestors that was never expressed. This deeply stored grief might also connect with a collective grief many are aware of these days that is in response to what has been lost globally.

If you are feeling the weight of the world plus your own personal grief, it might be important to get out in the beauty of nature, and let it nourish you. When we reconnect with Nature we find a source of hope and restoration. Nature reveals the continual cycle of life and death and renewal.

FINDING SUPPORT

Grieving all of the losses mentioned above means we need a "tribe," a community who will be there for us with loving compassion and intimacy. You might find this in a grief support group, a church, family, or some other group. You might have to begin with one friend and build from this. This is important because...

we need each other now more than ever!

A PARENT'S GRIEF

If your child has died I can imagine no greater pain than what you are experiencing. You may not feel you can survive it. You might feel paralyzed, shocked, or outraged: "This cannot be—children bury parents, NOT the other way around! Something is terribly wrong with the Universe or God to let this happen!" It is inconceivable!

It might seem impossible for your life to continue without your child. For awhile all will be "on hold." Progress through this sorrow will be in very tiny increments. It is a small step forward, perhaps, to even be looking at this book.

A marriage can be severely tested by this deepest sorrow. Sometimes each parent is in so much pain they find it difficult to reach out to the other. Suffering privately to "protect" their partner can feel like the loving thing to do. Yet, it is so important to stay connected by holding each other, offering a tender touch, listening, talking, doing daily tasks as a team, deciding things together, saying directly what you need, asking for help, and remembering that neither of you can fix this for the other or stop their pain.

There is help available. The Compassionate Friends offers grief support groups for parents. Go to http://www.compassionatefriends.org to find a local group. Of course, you might have strong support from extended family, church or temple friends, and other groups. Also consider individual and couples' counseling.

A child's death at any age, including pre-birth or an adult child, brings grief that is never really finished, but over time *it will ease*, held always in the depths of your heart.

How Do We Help Ourselves Through This Journey of Grief?

Although there are no right or wrong ways to grieve and no way to make it easy, there are some things we can do to help ourselves consciously grieve and move through it well. As you consider these ways listed in the next few pages be aware that doing them with the support of trusted friends or family is the ideal. It also may be that you find yourself doing many of them alone.

1. **Honor your feelings and who (or what) you have lost.**

Be deliberate and conscious about your grieving. Set your intention to honor all of your feelings and to honor the one you love and have lost. Allow yourself to be human with a human response.

2. **Make time and a place for grieving.**

Create a private place to spend time each day, as often as you need to stop and listen to your insides. Feel and express your feelings. Use whatever objects help focus and get you in touch with your feelings. Writing in this place might be very helpful. The main thing is showing up with the intention to grieve.

3. Expect and acknowledge triggers.

Anniversaries, birthdays, smells, sounds, memories, photos, places, songs, tastes, anything associated with your loved one, can bring them suddenly into clear focus again, This can bring on a new flood of intense feelings. Tears may flow. You might find it difficult to concentrate on whatever is in front of you. This is a time to stop, if possible, and take a break to let yourself release the emotions coming up. By talking about it, journaling, crying, being held—whatever feels right—you allow yourself to move through the feelings.

4. Express your feelings however you need to... or not.

Crying, moaning, groaning, yelling, calling out the name of your loved one... all are wholly natural responses. Punch a pillow, curl up in a ball, or just sit quietly... it is YOUR grief and there's no wrong way to do it as long as you keep your focus on your loss and maintain personal safety. An important part of this is having others create a "safe container" by their presence. This expression might happen spontaneously or you might, with your support group, create a more structured "grief ritual."

What if I can't cry? I feel like I should, but I just can't!

It's okay. Sometimes the tears just won't come. Some people do their grieving very quietly and inwardly. For some, emotions come out much later, when a person finally feels they can relax. Sometimes another loss comes along and opens the gates. How you do this is how you do it.

5. Comfort Yourself Lovingly

Sometimes your loved one's clothing, jewelry or other personal items will be strong triggers of memories, connection and comfort. For some it's too painful to have those things present. You might smell your loved one in a favorite shirt or sweater, or be comforted by having their watch on your dresser, or hat hanging in the hallway. Friends or family might encourage a quick "cleaning out" of closets and drawers, but you can take your time in deciding when to let go of things and, of course, you may hold on to some keepsakes forever.

6. Ask For What You Need

You might not be sure about what you need. Maybe all you can do is ask someone to come over and sit with you, or hold you, or NOT touch you. You might want to try out options to see what helps or doesn't. It could be a great help if someone simply came over and did your laundry or dishes or walked the dog. A very important part of staying well is to realize this is not a solo trip. Grief is part of us all and we need the support of a "tribe" or community to embrace and express it. When you share your grief with others you allow them to open their hearts to their own sorrow and to grow in their compassion.

If someone offers anything that is NOT helpful, it is perfectly fine to say, "Thanks, but that is not what I need right now." You might have reactions similar to the ones in the thought bubbles below. What might you ask for instead?

7. If angry, express and release it as soon as you can.

Your first reaction to loss might be to get very angry and to blame somebody.

You might even find you are angry at your loved one for dying, as irrational as that may seem.

Your anger might be aimed at God or whatever power you believe is in control of these things. It's important to express this and then move into the hurt and sadness.

8. Forgive yourself for regrets and shoulds.

If only I had spent more time with her. I'm so sorry for neglecting her!

I should have been there when he died!

The shoulds can be heavy burdens. Let them go soon.

Getting to forgiveness and compassion for ourselves is important so we can move on into our true grieving process. Guilt and self-punishment takes our energy and time and ultimately only makes us feel bad. They don't change the past or the fact we have lost someone. Getting to forgiveness of others can be challenging sometimes because of certain complications, as we shall see.

9. Give Yourself a Break

NOTICE

You might already be aware of how exhausting grieving can be to your mind, spirit and body. It is important to allow yourself a break from the pain and sadness, to shift your focus to something that relaxes, renews and lightens you. Dig in the garden, pet the dog, listen to the birds, sketch, wash the car, dance, play cards. At first, you might only be able to do it for brief moments, but even that can help. It will get easier as time passes.

10. Commemorate Your Loss

When you're ready, honor your loved one with a ritual or ceremony. Involve your whole self, body, mind, spirit, and your community. Plant a tree in memory of...

or express your love with a song, have a memorial celebration, write memories and appreciation in a poem or prose and post it to family and friends. Let your heart tell you what to do and when.

11. Invite Peace In

If guilt, regrets, anger, or resentment have got you in a dark place, stop. Breathe. Look out your window. Go out into some natural beauty. See if you can find one thing you are grateful for. Look for an opportunity to be kind or to receive some kindness. A simple smile or the song of a bird might be enough to shift your focus and outlook. All your emotions are valid. Sometimes, though, it is good to say, "I've been sad, or angry, or guilty enough for today. Time to let myself feel better."

How are you doing?

Grading yourself on how well you're grieving is not really a goal here, but it's good to be self-aware. You are probably okay if you are not seriously neglecting your basic needs, like food, water, sleep, warmth, personal hygiene. It's also a good sign that you're okay if you are allowing family or friends to support you and help with chores or errands. Grief is unpredictable and it wouldn't be unusual to experience moments, or even days, of feeling "normal" and able to function like your non-grieving self. Just remember grief is not neat and tidy. If you allow yourself to fully grieve, it's likely to be messy. People might not be comfortable and want you to control yourself, to keep your feelings inside. Choose people to be with who can truly support you and can tolerate the mess.

You might need some professional help...

...if you've stayed in bed for several days, or you're not eating, or using alcohol and/or drugs, or ignoring calls, or isolating for long periods, or thinking about suicide, then you need to talk with someone who is knowledgeable and trustworthy.
See the next page for possible options.

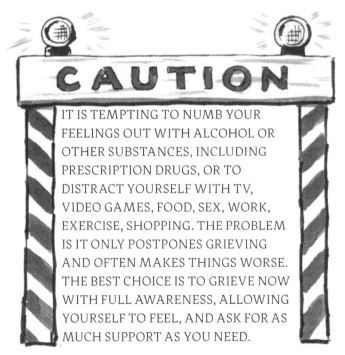

CAUTION

IT IS TEMPTING TO NUMB YOUR FEELINGS OUT WITH ALCOHOL OR OTHER SUBSTANCES, INCLUDING PRESCRIPTION DRUGS, OR TO DISTRACT YOURSELF WITH TV, VIDEO GAMES, FOOD, SEX, WORK, EXERCISE, SHOPPING. THE PROBLEM IS IT ONLY POSTPONES GRIEVING AND OFTEN MAKES THINGS WORSE. THE BEST CHOICE IS TO GRIEVE NOW WITH FULL AWARENESS, ALLOWING YOURSELF TO FEEL, AND ASK FOR AS MUCH SUPPORT AS YOU NEED.

What kind of help should I seek?

If you are having thoughts of suicide that persist you need to call someone now. Look for a mental health center in your area, a suicide prevention hotline, or call 911 if you feel unsafe. If suicide is not an immediate risk, but you definitely feel stuck in depression, exhaustion, substance abuse, or are simply unable to function, call a trusted friend or family member. Ask them to help you find a professional grief counselor. The counselor should have a degree in counseling, a license (required in most states), and experience in dealing with loss and grief. You might have to interview several to find a good fit and you might need someone to go with you to help. If you have a priest, rabbi, or minister who you trust, they, too, might be a source of help. Many communities have grief support groups which could also help. Online help: The Dougy Center, National Center for Grieving Children and Families, www.dougy.org.

If you choose to see your medical doctor or psychiatrist (who is also an MD), for help managing your grief, you will likely be given prescription drugs, such as an anti-depressant, tranquilizer, anti-anxiety medication or a sleep aid. You might be given one or a combination of these. Some psychologists are also able to prescribe certain drugs. Certainly, the vast majority of professionals want to relieve suffering and believe the best way is through medications. It is also true that there are times when medication is needed and very helpful. If you are extremely depressed, anxious, suicidal, not eating or sleeping, or sleeping all the time, and any of this has continued for several days, it is possible that medication could be part of what is needed. Medication without other treatment such as counseling is almost never a good choice. What I encourage you to be is proactive in your own grieving and consider this:

Grief is not an illness for which you need a cure.

It is a normal, healthy human response to a loss. If you are grieving deeply it means you have loved deeply. You are going to feel sad. You will be upset. You are a human, alive and feeling the loss. Allow yourself your feelings.

What If...

the person who died hurt you? Sometimes death takes someone before issues can be worked out with them.

I'm actually not sad that he's gone.

Sometimes, if the relationship was abusive, the feelings coming up are too painful, intense or confusing to deal with on your own. This is the time to seek professional help from someone skilled in these issues.

If Only...

Sometimes we need something from the person that was never offered, perhaps a parent's approval or a sibling's forgiveness. Or we want a relationship that we never had. These are issues that can intensify our grieving and make it very important to acknowledge feelings and share with someone we trust. If you hear yourself saying, "If only I had done...", then work on forgiving yourself as soon as you can and stop punishing yourself.

Unfinished Business

Your current loss might trigger other losses and other unfinished business such as old resentments, unhealed hurts, unmet needs, questions, feelings never expressed, apologies never spoken, forgiveness never offered. Now might be the opportunity to "clean out the closet" of your heart and lighten your emotional load. Take your time. Be gentle, honest and thorough. Ask for help from someone you trust who has skills to guide and support you.

More on Forgiveness

If the person who died abused, abandoned, neglected, or hurt you in some other way, you may find it hard to forgive them. You might not even WANT to forgive them. That's okay. At some point you could decide you are tired of feeling angry and carrying around the resentment. You might fear that letting it go would be like saying what the person did to you was okay. But forgiveness is not about condoning conduct. It is not really for the other person—they are dead after all. It is for YOU. You didn't deserve to be hurt and you don't deserve to suffer over this now. You can choose, when ready, to let your anger go and be free of this toxic burden. This could take some time and you will probably need help working through it.

Dealing with Suicide

Many people feel suicide is the most difficult kind of loss because it is like a "double pain"—grieving the loss of your loved one's presence and the reality that they chose to die. You might be feeling guilty, questioning whether or not you could have prevented it, or angry—how could they do this to you!? How could they just give up on life? It's impossible to really know the particular pain your loved one might have been suffering or how they arrived at the choice they made. There is no way of knowing if anything could have saved them. Grieving means wrestling with these questions which may never be answered. But, from the deep well of your heart's grief can come great compassion for both your loved one and yourself. This will take time.

Violent Death

If your loved one was the victim of a violent death then you face the difficult challenge of handling the inevitable feelings towards the perpetrator of the violence. You will probably have to deal with whatever legal proceedings might go on for a long time. This can be very taxing and you will need as much support as you can get. Be gentle with yourself and ask for help each step of the way.

Eventually

you will be aware of moving from the tough feelings, like sorrow and depression, to brighter, more hopeful ones.

The waves of emotion may still roll in at unpredictable times, triggered by any number of things that connect to your loss, but they won't be so intense and powerful...

Happier Feelings

will begin to return and replace the sorrow and sadness in your heart. The ability to feel joy and excitement about life will gradually come back, along with physical energy, desires, creativity, interests and hopefulness. You're likely to find yourself making plans and connecting with people more, and eating and sleeping much better.

Grieving Fully

rarely means that you will reach a point where there is no more grief. Certain triggers might continue to set off some moments of grieving. You can always choose to honor yourself by acknowledging your feelings, taking time out, doing what feels right for you, then moving back into life again with love and gratitude.

The Ultimate Questions

If your loved one has died, you might be asking: Where are they now? Is there life after death? Can I communicate with them? Is there a way to really know if they're all right? It's very natural to have these questions. Talking about them with a trusted spiritual leader might be very helpful.

There are many books and resources offering deep explorations of this topic. I encourage you to investigate these for yourself. Doing a search online by typing in "life after death" will render a large number of resources. You may find material that doesn't fit with you at all, some that is comforting and consistent with your own experience, faith and understanding, and some that may be equally comforting by opening you to ideas you may not have previously considered. In all, I believe the search could be beneficial.

Do's and Don'ts for helping someone who is grieving...

1. Show up and be present. Listen, be still, use words sparingly. There is little that can be said at the time of loss that is truly helpful. Don't say, "I know just how you feel" because you don't. Your presence speaks volumes.
2. Ask what they need, but be aware they might not know.
3. Offer practical help like making phone calls, watching the children, feeding the dog, etc.
4. Encourage expression of their feelings, even if you are uncomfortable with it. Don't console or wipe away their tears. Don't try to cheer them up! Just create a safe space.
5. Sit near them and hold their hand, if they consent.
6. Keep showing up over time because often the most difficult time is several weeks after a loss.
7. Be aware of your own emotional state while supporting the others. It is easy for our own losses and grief to be triggered as we deal with someone else's. If this happens, follow the guidelines in this book and get support.

The compassion you offer someone might make all the difference.

Signs that someone might need more help than you alone can provide:

- Long periods of isolation
- Not caring for their physical needs for several days
- Suicidal thoughts and talk
- Serious symptoms of depression present for several days (low energy, withdrawn, tearful, sleeping a lot, no appetite, suicidal thoughts, hopeless feeling)
- Being stuck in one emotion for an extended time
- Total denial of any loss, escaping into distractions
- Frequent use of alcohol or drugs to numb feelings

See page 39 for ideas about the kind of help to seek.

A Quick Guide to
GRIEF TENDING

1. Realize my emotions won't be predictable.

2. Honor my feelings by making a space and time to be with my grief each day.

3. Acknowledge and express my feelings in whatever ways work for me.

4. Ask for friends/family support and say what helps, what doesn't.

5. Talk about my loss to people I trust to listen lovingly.

6. Eat healthy food daily and drink lots of water. (Grieving people tend to get dehydrated.)

7. Get regular exercise and rest.

8. Get outside often and connect with nature.

9. Allow myself to take breaks from sadness, to laugh and relax.

10. Commemorate the loss with a ceremony of my own design.

11. Since there are no right or wrong ways to grieve I will not judge myself for how I do it.

12. Be patient with how long my grieving takes.

13. When memories get triggered, focus on the gratitude I have for the one I have lost.

14. Breathe and give myself permission to live and be happy.

About the Author/Illustrator

Jack Wiens, M.A., has been a licensed professional counselor for over 30 years. He received his degree from Azusa Pacific College in southern California. He has worked in private practice, inpatient and outpatient addiction treatment, and was director of bereavement and training in a hospice program for four years. He is also an accomplished artist. This booklet teams his clinical experience with his artistic gift in a unique way to address a subject for which he has deep passion and compassion.

Jack lives in Ashland, Oregon, not far from where he was born. He enjoys creating art and teaching it, exploring the natural beauty of the area, and growing the close relationships with his tribe of friends. He has two grown children and three grandchildren.

Visit his website at www.jackwiens.com.

Acknowledgements

I want to thank all the friends and loved ones who read the first drafts of this book and offered wise and valuable feedback. Also, huge thanks to Neale Donald Walsch for his caring input. Thank you Patty Arnold for your wonderful design work. And thank you to the Haines & Friends Foundation for supporting this project with your grant. Finally, I want to thank all the dear people who came in my counseling office over the years, shared their sorrow, and taught me about grief.

Recommended Reading:
The Wild Edge of Sorrow by Francis Weller
Honoring Grief by Alexandra Kennedy

Made in the USA
San Bernardino, CA
27 September 2016